UNSEEN
NEWCASTLE-
UNDER-LYME

UNSEEN NEWCASTLE-UNDER-LYME

NEIL COLLINGWOOD

The History Press

First published 2014

The History Press
The Mill, Brimscombe Port
Stroud, Gloucestershire, GL5 2QG
www.thehistorypress.co.uk

British Library Cataloguing in Publication Data.
A catalogue record for this book is available from the British Library.

ISBN 978 0 7509 5598 0

Typesetting and origination by The History Press
Printed in Great Britain

CONTENTS

Acknowledgements   6

Introduction   7

1   The Castle Street Development   9

2   Lost Villages   15

3   Newcastle Town Centre   31

4   Big Houses   55

5   Lost Houses, Lost Streets   67

6   Full Steam Ahead   79

7   Changing Scenery   87

8   People and Events   95

9   Newcastle Brown, Anyone?   107

10 Pick 'n' Mix   115

ACKNOWLEDGEMENTS

I would like to thank all the staff and volunteers at Newcastle Borough Museum, notably: Delyth Copp, Teresa Mason, Vanessa Griffiths, Clare Griffiths, Emma Reardon, Leanne Worrall, Gwyneth Pearson, Stan Mayer and Jim Worgan. Also Robert Foster at Newcastle-under-Lyme Borough Council, Newcastle-under-Lyme Civic Society, G.A.B.S. Shufflebotham, Nicholas and Norma Hill, Peter and Karen Kaminski, Reverend Martin R. Connop-Price, the Hickton family, Nick Wood and Porthill Scouts, Peter Hand, Beamish Museum, Paul Jarman, Anne Brockley, and Bill Byatt and Stuart Richards at Wolstanton Hardware.

Photographs marked JWC (Jim Wain Collection) are reproduced by permission of Newcastle-under-Lyme Civic Society. The Jim Wain Collection is now held in Newcastle-under-Lyme Borough Museum & Art Gallery but the reproduction rights rest with Newcastle-under-Lyme Civic Society.

INTRODUCTION

Unseen Newcastle-under-Lyme is compiled from old photographs of the Borough of Newcastle and has been created with two very particular aims in mind: firstly, it unashamedly advertises Newcastle-under-Lyme Borough Museum & Art Gallery and demonstrates the qualities and virtues of the museum's photographic collection. The collection consists of many thousands of images covering every aspect of life in the borough as far back as the 1850s; it also contains many portraits of local people, some famous and some very ordinary but, regardless of their status, all are someone's parents, grandparents or ancestors. Most of the images from the collection can be made available to enhance family histories, to illustrate historical projects or simply to display in the home or workplace. How fascinating it is to discover an old photograph of your own house taken fifty or a hundred years ago and to see the people who were living there then.

Secondly – and here the title provides a clue – the book seeks to excite admirers of old Newcastle photographs, even those who already own every Newcastle book published previously. To this end the author, in collaboration with the museum staff, has gathered together a selection of images that is unusual for a variety of reasons. The first group is unusual because the images have been acquired by the museum relatively recently. Some have been in private ownership for a century or more and so have never had the opportunity to be published before. Examples of this are the many photographs taken by Newcastle Borough Council's Planning Department of areas due to be cleared in the 1930s–1950s and 1960s. Sadly most of these photographs are almost devoid of people, clearly a deliberate council policy, but despite that they are often amongst very few surviving images of certain long-gone streets: Bath Street, Mortimore Street, Hart Street, Hall Street, etc.

Another group of photographs that was acquired a few years ago had been taken by the proprietor of Colin Smith's shop in Bridge Street to record the areas of Liverpool Road, Bridge Street, Broad Street, etc. prior to the wholesale demolition that took place in those areas when the A34 ring road was created. Even more recent acquisitions are the superb and invaluable photographs taken or collected by the late Jim Wain of Wain's Chemist's. This collection has been made available to the museum by the generosity of Newcastle-under-Lyme Civic Society (who retain the reproduction rights) and contain such gems as the only known colour photograph of the old Globe Commercial Hotel in Red Lion Square. Another group are the personal and family photographs taken by Newcastle residents, rather than being postcard-type images. Photographing certain scenes almost dictate a particular spot where a professional photographer stands and so certain viewpoints have been repeated almost ad nauseam, whilst other buildings or streets seldom, if ever, appear. Family photos of shops or houses often break this convention and show buildings or backgrounds unseen anywhere before. An example of this is the photograph of a Corpus Christi procession in Bridge Street, taken simply because a relative of the photographer was taking part. In the background can clearly be seen The New Vine public house, complete with the name of the licensee, the only image of this pub the author has ever seen.

Finally, there are photographs selected simply because of the difficulties that they presented in making them suitable for use, meaning they probably wouldn't or couldn't have ever been published previously. This group includes glass negatives of various sizes that have been scratched or even dropped and broken. The front cover photograph is one of three such large glass negatives that were donated by the same person, having apparently had something heavy placed on them that had broken them all into two or three pieces. There are old prints that have been torn, scuffed, defaced or allowed to fade, but which have been painstakingly brought back to a reasonable condition.

Because of the intention to present views that have been unseen previously, a few of the images used in the book are not of the highest quality but if they are not, they will have been selected because they are at worst very unusual and at best unique.

Whilst the original intention was to only include previously unpublished photographs, it has become apparent that amongst less mainstream and more specialist publications, a few of them have appeared before. It also became obvious that one or two photographs that had appeared in general Newcastle photograph books had to be used again for reasons of completeness. The first chapter (The Castle Street Development) would have been most unsatisfactory had it not contained a single photograph of Castle Street itself and only using previously unpublished photographs would have led to this result. The author still hopes that the vast majority of the images will be completely unknown to collectors of Newcastle books.

I hope that you will enjoy the book and find the images interesting and possibly look further into aspects of the borough's history. Sales will help to support the services provided by the Borough Museum and hopefully encourage more people to use the photographic (and archive) collection. If this volume proves popular, perhaps there may be a second volume later.

Grateful thanks are offered to the staff and volunteers at the museum, Newcastle-under-Lyme Borough Council, Newcastle-under-Lyme Civic Society and all of those individuals and organisations who have donated images to the collection. Without donations the collection would not exist, so please contact the author or the museum if you feel that you may have some images that have not been seen before and would be worthy of inclusion in a book like this one. Even if you do not wish to donate the original photograph, the museum would be grateful for the opportunity to make a digital copy of it.

Neil Collingwood, 2014

1

THE CASTLE STREET DEVELOPMENT

The Clarence public house, Clarence Street.

By 1840 a new working-class grid-plan housing development had been laid out adjacent to George Street. Centred on Castle Street, it stretched from Marsh Parade in the west to Boundary Street in the east. The eastern edge of Boundary Street formed the Parliamentary and Municipal boundary between Newcastle-under-Lyme and Stoke-upon-Trent, meaning that the development lay just within Newcastle. The same boundary line still divides Newcastle from Stoke-on-Trent today.

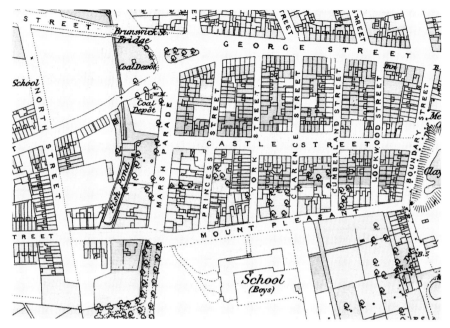

Map of Castle Street development. This old estate map shows the Castle Street development, to the south of which is the boys' school built in 1874, which would later be called Newcastle High School. The fishpond near Marsh Parade was a surviving fragment of the old upper canal, which the railway was built over and which terminated in what is now Stubbs' Walks. The Castle Street development was almost entirely demolished in 1958.

Castle Street, 1957. This photograph of Castle Street looking towards the Clarence public house shows where the section of the street between Princess Street and Clarence Street was built disproportionately wide in order to accommodate a street market. There is no record that such a market ever actually took place, however: residents presumably still preferred to walk into town to shop on the Stones.

Castle Street, 1957. The photographer crossed Castle Street to take this image, which shows the junction of Clarence Street and Castle Street. Further along Castle Street can be seen at the end of Cumberland Street. These streets, together with York Street, were named after the royal dukes of the early Victorian period. Like most housing developments, the Castle Street area had its own pubs and shops and it was clearly intended that the development could be largely independent of Newcastle town centre.

Boundary Street, 1957. Boundary Street was so named because its eastern edge formed the boundary between the Borough of Newcastle and neighbouring Stoke-upon-Trent. The street used to stretch from George Street to the top end of Mount Pleasant and was lined by terraced houses. Today it is home to No. 1 Boundary Street and the former Mount Zion Methodist Chapel, now Newcastle Christian Fellowship. Beyond that the road becomes a lawn surrounding one of the blocks of flats that now cover the area.

Princess Street from George Street, 1957. The first road above Marsh Parade to cross Castle Street was Princess Street or, to give it the name it had when it was built, Princes Street. Today it is the only one of the original five cross-streets to still follow its original course. The shops on both corners still stand, the former Copes' motorcycle showroom now selling motorcycle clothing. The terraces have all gone, with just one house standing between Castle Street and Mount Pleasant.

Princess Street from Castle Street, 1957. Taken across Castle Street, this second photo shows the Mount Pleasant end of Princess Street, its corner shop formed from part of the silk mill in Marsh Parade. This mill survives today but has been leased for various purposes at least since the 1960s. When this photo was taken there was a mix of terraced houses and yards in Princess Street but today the street contains only a car park, some lock-up garages and a single surviving detached house.

York Street from Castle Street, 1957. This is the view from Castle Street, along York Street towards Mount Pleasant. In the distance is the front door of what was then Newcastle High School, now part of Newcastle-under-Lyme Independent School. On the corner is W. Lowe's grocer's shop with the obligatory advertising for cigarettes, Cherry Blossom Polish and Colman's mustard.

Clarence Street from Castle Street, 1957. This section of Clarence Street has no corner shop but a bit of life is imparted by the fact that the postman has parked his bicycle against the wall on the right and is delivering to a business on the left. In the background is the roof of the old high school laboratories and the tall wall running along Lancaster Road against which the school's Combined Cadet Force (CCF) buildings stood.

Lockwood Street from George Street, 1957. On the left of this photo is the door to the bar of the Alma Inn. The Alma is still pulling pints, despite standing isolated since all of its neighbours were demolished decades ago. On the right is S.T. Chadwick's Radio Spares shop, which moved to new premises on the opposite side of George Street when the shop shown here was demolished.

George Street, the northern edge of the development, 1954. Taken from opposite Marsh Parade this shot of Copes' motorcycle dealers also shows the ends of the Castle Street development's cross streets. These can be seen between the shops that stretch all the way up George Street. Today there are only a couple of original properties above Princess Street and everything else up to the Alma Inn has been demolished. The resulting gap was filled by Andrew Place, built in the 1960s, and its car park.

2

LOST VILLAGES

Leycett from a distance.

The lost villages of the title include Longbridge Hayes and Leycett, former mining villages that were demolished once their reason for existing had disappeared. Also included is a third village, the Higherland, once completely separate from Newcastle. Although the Higherland still exists today, it has been changed beyond recognition and swallowed up by the expansion of the town.

Keele Estate map of Longbridge Hayes. Longbridge Hayes was a small community at the end of Longbridge Hayes Road consisting of three streets: John Street, Peel Street and Cross Street. Cross Street ran along the bottom of John Street and across Peel Street and there was originally one further terrace of larger houses called Church View. If it survived today, Longbridge Hayes would be sandwiched between the West Coast Mainline and the A500 D-Road, beneath which lie any surviving remnants of Church View.

Cross Street, Longbridge Hayes, 1980. This 1980 view shows the full length of Cross Street with the end of John Street in the foreground and the end of Peel Street in the distance. A Cross Street does still exist in the area today but is now just an access road into the Longbridge Hayes Industrial Estate. The boundary line between Newcastle and Stoke-on-Trent lies at the edge of Longbridge Hayes Road, meaning that Longbridge Hayes fell just inside the Borough of Newcastle.

Peel Street, Longbridge Hayes, 1980. This view is looking down Peel Street towards Cross Street. At least two shops are visible; one on the corner and another, five doors lower down. A Primitive Methodist Chapel was built on the corner of Peel Street and Cross Street in 1879 and was still in use in 1957. The last houses to be demolished in Longbridge Hayes were the row of terraces on one side of Peel Street in 1988.

Peel Street, Longbridge Hayes, 1980. This photo shows the top few houses in Peel Street. The typical arrangement of terraced streets can be seen here where at intervals along the row there was an alleyway to the 'backs'. These alleyways, often referred to on deeds as 'wheelbarrow roads', would originally have allowed the 'night-soil' man with his barrow access to the outside toilets that all of these houses would have had when built.

John Street, Longbridge Hayes, 1980. On different maps the building at top right of John Street, (shown here), is marked either as St Wulstan's Mission church or simply as 'School'. According to the *Victoria County History*, Longbridge Hayes National School in John Street, Longbridge Hayes was built in 1871 but we know from the interior photograph of St Wulstan's (*see* next photo) that it was still operating as a church in 1913. It must therefore be assumed that the building served as both church and school.

Inside St Wulstan's church, John Street, Longbridge Hayes, 1913. This is the interior of St Wulstan's Mission church. Two of the altar servers were brothers: Colin and Alfred Jackson lived in John Street in 1911 with their mother Agnes and their sister Ada. Agnes had lost two of her five children in their childhood, followed by her husband. Within a few years of this photo being taken, the First World War took both Colin and Alfred – such a great weight of sorrow in one small family.

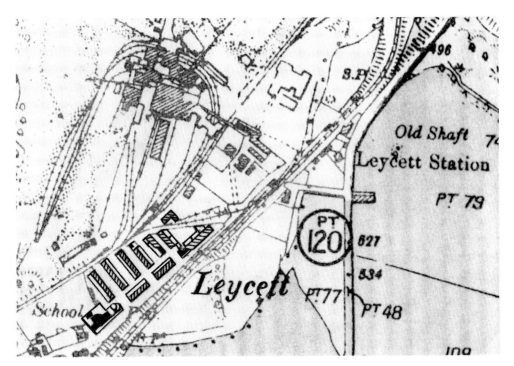

Keele Estate sale map of Leycett, 1951. This sale catalogue map shows that Leycett was not a typical village stretched along a country road, but rather resembled a small town plonked in the middle of nowhere. It had been built for mining families by Lord Crewe in 1868 and had its own school, church, shops and off-licence. The crest of the Crewe family occupied the gable in the centre of one of the Front Street terraces. The village was levelled in 1968/69 and permission was refused to rebuild the village in 1975.

Front Street, Leycett, 1964.
These two young lads with their cart pose for the photographer Revd Martin R. Connop-Price, with Front Street behind them. The houses in the centre are empty, with their downstairs doors and windows bricked up and the upstairs windows smashed. The houses to the left and right are still occupied and a remaining elderly resident peers from an upstairs window, perhaps thinking back on happier times and wondering how long he might be able to remain in his home.

Older residents, Front Street, Leycett, 1964. Rather older than the previous two subjects, these Leycett residents stand at the side of Leycett Lane with the school/church and the village/miners' hall behind them. To their right was the first of the three terraces forming Front Street, one of which was called Railway Terrace. The streets in Leycett were imaginatively called Top Street, Bottom Street and, between them, Middle Street. Along the end of these three was Front Street.

When's the next one due? Front Street, Leycett, 1964. A PMT double-decker bus trundles along Leycett Lane, past the shop on the corner of Middle Street and the terraces. It would then pass where the two old gentlemen above were standing and then the school/church. Some of the houses were clearly still lived in and there is still a set of scales in the shop. It is strange to think that there is virtually no trace today that this thriving community ever existed.

Meet me on the corner ... Leycett, 1964. In this photo, a group of women of all ages cluster around the steps of the shop at the corner of Front Street and Middle Street. It is difficult to know whether they would have done this normally or whether they were persuaded to do so by the photographer. Next door to the corner shop was Mr Walter Lawton's Off Licence selling alcohol which was 'Not to be consumed on the premises'.

Locomotive *Lena* at Leycett, 11 September 1954. In this photo the 0-6-0ST (saddle tank) locomotive *Lena* sits idle at Leycett. Together with *Madeley*, *Lena* was a Leycett Colliery locomotive. Not only did the village have railway lines adjacent to it but there was also a station there, so that miners from further afield could travel to work at the 'Bang-up' or 'Fair Lady' pits. Why could the streets in Leycett not have been as imaginatively named as the collieries?

Leycett, 1964. This view was taken from the area behind the terraces in Front Street looking across Middle Street and was obviously used as a place for residents to park their cars (if they had one). The three small children are standing by the rear wall of the corner shop with its interesting miniature industrial chimney. The lady in the apron watching her dog also appeared on the photo of the corner shop on page 21.

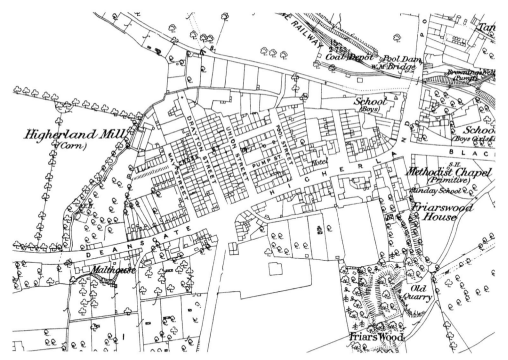

Map of the Higherland and surroundings. Although the Higherland has long been a suburb of Newcastle rather than a separate village, when the streets were first laid out there would have been nothing around them but open fields. The development had its own pubs, shops, and places of worship. In the late 1960s almost every original building was demolished, notable survivors being The Sneyd Arms public house and the terraced house at the top of Drayton Street, now incorporated into the pub.

Friarswood from Seabridge Road, 1920s. Seabridge Road originally ran through a cutting, one side of which survives as a raised terrace lined by semi-detached houses. Opposite was a dry-stone wall behind which were allotment gardens several feet above the road. This view by Thomas Pape was taken from those allotments. Seabridge Road was the main route from Newcastle to Whitmore until the late 1920s, when Priory Road was created by cutting through the sandstone to the east of Friarswood.

Medieval trackway, the Higherland, 1920s. This photograph taken by Pape shows a medieval trackway which led from Friarswood towards Seabridge. Ordnance Survey maps show it going from Friarswood to an old quarry before apparently stopping, although perhaps it just became less obvious and so is not shown on the maps. The trackway would have roughly followed the terrace on the right-hand side of Priory Road as you travel uphill towards the Westlands. Friarswood probably only survives because of its deep disused stone quarry.

Ashley's Higherland Cash Stores, 1960s. The Higherland Cash Stores, simply known by locals as Ashley's, stood on the corner of Pool Street and Higherland, which is actually the name of the main road. It was an Aladdin's cave of produce, the forerunner of the supermarket, with items of all descriptions hanging from or standing on every inch of the shop, except for a small area where customers stood to be served. The date stone high on the corner reads '1802'.

Eardley's Confectioners and Tobacconist, 1960s. Eardley's stood on the opposite side of the Higherland from Ashley's and attempted to maintain a slightly more dignified appearance. Although modernised and ostensibly a confectioner and tobacconist, the window can be seen to contain Scott's Porridge Oats, Heinz soups, Bovril and what may be a card of watch straps. A few doors further down stood one of H. & E. Shaw's chain of newsagents and, below that, Patterson & Hall's builders' yard.

Montgomery's shop, Deansgate, June 1961. Montgomery's was further along the main road than the other shops, on a stretch of the road called Deansgate. Deansgate still exists on modern maps, although a Higherland sign has recently been incorrectly erected near to Marson's Garage. This seems to be something that regularly causes confusion though, because the next photo claims to have been taken from Keele Road but was actually taken from Deansgate.

Opposite above: **Union Street, 1960s.** This is the view down Union Street towards Pool Dam Playing Fields. On the right is the end of Pump Street and, below that, Cross Street. These houses have the stepped window lintels so typical of the Georgian houses built in this area in the late eighteenth–early nineteenth century. This ties in with the date stone of 1802 on Ashley's shop at the top of Pool Street.

Opposite below: **View along Higherland towards May Street, June 1961.** This view, looking towards Keele, shows the right-hand side of the road from the Sneyd Arms to May Street and beyond to Montgomery's shop in Deansgate (*see* above). When the area was cleared, May Street and Cross Street, which crossed it, were completely eliminated. In the distance can just be seen the Thistleberry Arms a public house built just behind the site of Thistleberry House (*see* Big Houses).

View of Newcastle from Deansgate, 1940. This highly unusual view was taken from roughly opposite where B.S. Marson's Garage stands today. It shows Higherland Corn Mill and, to the right of that, the end of Cross Street. In the distance from left to right are Holborn Paper Mill, St Giles' church, St George's church, the Globe Commercial Hotel (Red Lion Square) and the Municipal Hall. The hoarding to the left of the Mill Chimney advertises Lifebuoy Soap, still available today. No 'Smoke Control Zone', this.

3

NEWCASTLE TOWN CENTRE

The Globe Hotel, Red Lion Square.

Towns change more rapidly than villages as changes in lifestyle dictate changes to roads and buildings: more and larger vehicles require wider, straighter roads. Larger shops and supermarkets replace small shops. Town houses make way for more shops and older buildings are demolished to make way for new ones. Newcastle town centre has changed enormously in the past century, the biggest changes probably occurring in the 1960s. The photographs in this section give a taste of just how comprehensive these changes have been.

The Hind's Vaults, Red Lion Square. This is the building that stands at the right-hand edge of the previous photo. It was demolished as part of the second phase of the building of the York Place shopping centre. It seems strange to think that planning consent could be granted to demolish such an important piece of Newcastle's history in order to erect a modern shopping precinct. The original wattle and daub double gables were infilled with brick in 1843. (JWC)

The Three Tuns, Red Lion Square, 1950s. The building shown here is the Tudor Three Tuns public house, together with Halford's bicycle shop. The building was demolished in 1959 (presumably by Halford's, who built a new shop on the site), now the 'Art of Siam' Restaurant. This photo was taken by Jim Wain, possibly to capture the last days of the building in which his grandfather, Clement Wain, began his chemist's business prior to moving to the building still bearing his name. (JWC)

Red Lion Square, 1920s. This view from the junction of Ironmarket and High Street shows how dramatically the buildings have changed in Red Lion Square. On the right is the old main post office, which was demolished and replaced by a bank. Beyond that, every building on the right was demolished and replaced in the late 1960s. In front of Wain's chemist can be seen the old Weights and Measures office, with its underground gents' toilet. The office was demolished in 1926.

Church Street, around 1910. This photo is similar to others taken around the same time but is superior in that it gives a much clearer view of the buildings on the lower left side of Church Street, including the Ring of Bells pub, where John Wesley once preached from an upstairs window. It also shows the buildings on Lower Street opposite Church Street. In the bottom of Wain's window is an impressive stock of photographic equipment, including box and folding cameras. (JWC)

35

Tarmac laying in Red Lion Square, around 1926. This photo shows resurfacing work in Red Lion Square, which took place between 1926, when the weights and measures office was demolished, and 1928, when PET's electric trams were replaced by PMT buses. The machine in the foreground is probably for breaking up stone into suitably sized pieces to mix with bitumen to form tarmac. Behind that is the tarmac boiler and an early roadroller. The Globe Hotel and Goodwin's Printers are visible in the background. (JWC)

Tarmac laying in Red Lion Square, around 1926. This is the same occasion as the previous photo, but now looking south-east, towards the Guildhall. In the foreground wooden barrels of bitumen can be seen and on this image it can be seen that the tarmac boiler contains a motor-driven agitator to mix up the bitumen and stone ready for laying. It appears that the sun is just attempting to cut through an early morning fog. (JWC)

High Street from Red Lion Square, 1970s. This view shows the wholesale changes to the north end of High Street since the early 1980s. The Rex and Rio Cinemas stand empty but it can be seen that they occupied a mid-nineteenth-century building (Goodall's Furnishers). This was later demolished and replaced by Lloyd's Bank. Blockley's and Sketchley's were in Georgian buildings that have survived. Black's and Henry White's were originally the (new) Roebuck coaching inn and now only their frontages remain, converted into the Roebuck Centre.

Henry White's 'Ladies', Sutherland House, High Street, around 1968. Having been in business for more than eighty years, the passing of Henry White's was much lamented. It is said that Sutherland House was the last property in the town owned by the Trentham Estate; for 200 years, the Leveson/Leveson-Gower family had maintained their hold on Parliamentary control of Newcastle by purchasing virtually every rented property in the town. It was difficult to say no when your landlord said 'Vote for whom I say, or lose your home.' (JWC)

The Market Cross, 1950s. In this 1950s view of the market cross and part of High Street, Boots the Chemist is located in a relatively small Georgian building. Not long afterwards Massey's ironmongers would close and be incorporated into larger premises for Boots, with a ground floor and an upstairs where vinyl records could be listened to in booths equipped with headphones. The Georgian building occupied by Co-operative Footwear has also since been demolished and replaced.

High Street from Friars Street to the Roebuck Centre, 1972. This rainy photograph shows not only how buildings have been altered in Newcastle, but also how retail has changed. Although still a national business, Halford's has moved several times; Mac Fisheries went to the wall in 1979; Dewhurst's Butchers were finally dissolved in 2006; Lipton's Supermarkets were closed or rebranded in 1985 and Burgess' Blackfriars' Bakery, cafes and restaurants went into voluntary liquidation in 1996. Only Boots, much altered, still remains where it was in this photo.

Burgess' and Mandley & Unett, around 1970. This close up of part of the previous scene shows Burgess' York Café. At the front of the premises was the cake and pie shop, selling Burgess' own Blackfriars Bakery produce and behind that, down a few steps, was the Brunch Bar, where teenagers would meet after school. Upstairs was a rather more posh Burgess' restaurant and next door was Mandley and Unett's book and stationery shop.

Mandley & Unett's Stationers, High Street, 1964. Many people regret the passing of Mandley & Unett's shop. The fact that they had been in business for 260 years when this photograph was taken in 1964 meant that Newcastle shoppers were probably quite used to them being there. As well as selling books and stationery, Mandley & Unett were also printers and, at the rear of the shop, sold trainset accessories and Lego, some of which can be seen in the left-hand side of the window.

High Street and the Guildhall, 1960s. This early 1960s view shows Newcastle's High Street when it was still a traffic thoroughfare. The old Market Hall (1856) has been demolished and building the new Market Arcade (now the Vue Cinema) is awaited. The Lamb Inn has been demolished on the corner of Friar's Street and the new Maypole building is rising up in its place.

The Guildhall and Castle Hotel, 1930s. This photo was taken prior to the demolition of the old Roebuck coaching inn and the erection of the Art Deco Lancaster Buildings in 1936. To the left of the Castle Hotel (then owned by Trust House), J. Bagguley and Sons are at No. 23 High Street, then is the Globe Café, Home & Colonial, the Rainbow Inn (*see* Newcastle Brown, Anyone?), Johnson's cleaners and finally Mellard's ironmongers.

Demolition of the Castle Hotel, 1970s. A long battle was fought against the demolition of the Georgian Castle Hotel in High Street and eventually a compromise was reached to allow the conversion of the building to a form a suitable venue for modern retailing whilst still retaining the building's historic appearance and character. Unfortunately the demolition of the entire building except for the front wall, total reconstruction of the roof and alteration of the windows left very little of either the building's history or character.

Demolition of the Castle Hotel, 1970s. This view from Market Lane shows the rear of the Castle Hotel partway through its demolition. The old garage and other outbuildings have already been taken down and the roof stripped away. Soon nothing will stand except the front wall. To the left of the archway was a High Street shop with hotel bedrooms overhead. Scarlet Street on the left still exists and used to give access to High Street through a narrow passage.

National Provincial Bank, High Street, 1950s. The National Provincial, now the Natwest Bank, stands on the corner of High Street and Hassell Street. Originally it had two neighbours, which meant that access from Hassell Street to High Street was via a narrow entry – running where the pavement behind the market stall on the left of this photo is now. The building was originally a town house lived in by the Fenton and Fletcher families and was converted to a bank in the early 1900s.

Redman's, High Street, late 1960s. This photo shows Redman's self-service shop, an early supermarket in the pre-decimalisation late 1960s. John West's Red Salmon, Shredded Wheat and Nestlé's Cream could be bought here, with the price decreasing the more tins/packets that you bought. To the left of Redman's was N.W. Frost's butchers. The building occupied by Redman's probably dated from the 1950s or early 1960s and is today occupied by the Newcastle Branch of the Hanley Economic Building Society.

Old Bank House, High Street, 1972. Visible to the right of the National Provincial Bank in the photograph on the previous page, in its final years Old Bank House was occupied by the Borough Council's Education Department. In this photograph taken in 1972, George Hollins and Sons Ltd, ironmongers and N.W. Frost, butcher, have just been demolished and this property will soon follow to make way for the present Leeds House. Alderman A. Ryles wrote in 1960 that Old Bank House had once formed part of its larger Georgian neighbour.

George Hollins & Sons Ltd, late 1960s. George Hollins & Sons Ltd at one time had two shops in High Street including the one shown here. They were direct competitors of Mellard's and sold all manner of tools and equipment for builders, carpenters and plumbers. At Christmas, like various other specialist shops in the town, they also packed their windows with toys and games that they only stocked for a limited period each year. Here the shop has already closed and will soon be bought and demolished.

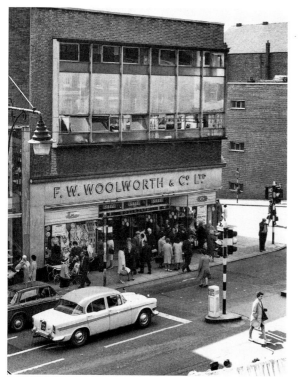

F.W. Woolworth's, High Street, 1960s. This view shows F.W. Woolworth's when even heavy goods vehicles still travelled through the town centre. The crossroads here was controlled by traffic lights and a serious accident happened on 9 July 1965, when a driver suffered a heart attack at the wheel and ploughed into the front of Woolworth's on a busy Saturday. Three people died and many more were injured. Today, relatively little motor traffic passes through this area.

The 'Sunken Gardens', 1960s. This roundabout with its gardens was created in 1964 and originally had the fountain shown at its centre. The fountain did not last long though, firstly being filled in and used as a flowerbed and then removed completely. This scene is very different today as the George Inn, visible on the right, and the row of shops on the left of Barracks' Road were pulled down in the 1980s to allow the road to be widened.

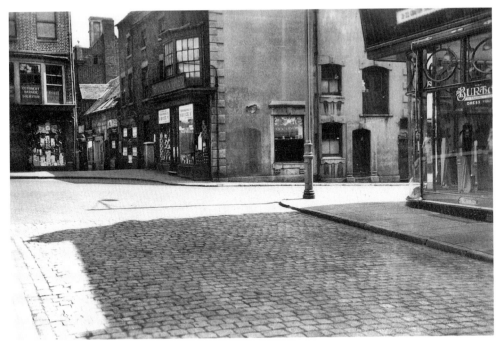

Cheapside from Ironmarket, around 1935. This photo, from the Jim Wain Collection, was recently deposited at the Borough Museum by Newcastle Civic Society. It is probably unique as it shows the entrance to Cheapside prior to the demolition of the old Roebuck inn in 1935. There are many views of this building but no others showing Cheapside in this way. The photograph was taken from Lad Lane and at this time the road to the right was not Ironmarket but New Street. (JWC)

Ironmarket from High Street, 1958. This photo shows a number of buildings no longer with us, the most obvious being the Municipal Hall, demolished in the mid-1960s. Also long gone is the cast-iron and glass arcade in front of Henry Whites and the tall building to the right of Swettenham's Café, almost opposite Henry White's. That particular building seems to have been one of the most camera-shy shops in the town. The old bus is en route to Chesterton from Hanley via Garner Street.

Henry White's, Ironmarket. This image of Henry White's Gents' Outfitter appears to have been taken at a time of great celebration, possibly for the Coronation of Queen Elizabeth II in 1953. Although the cast-iron arcade was removed many years ago, the Georgian building itself has survived. Sadly a selection of doors and windows of differing sizes and heights have been inserted into the ground floor, destroying the classical Georgian regularity of the building. (JWC)

Jaeger promotion, Henry White's. Here Henry White's men's shop in Ironmarket, under its arcade, is promoting Jaeger Pure Wool Clothing. Jaeger got its name from nineteenth-century German zoologist Dr Gustav Jaeger, who advocated the benefits of animal rather then vegetable fibres for clothing. The glass and cast-iron arcade survived until around 1970 and was a blessing for those waiting for buses at the main Hanley bus stop in wet weather. Today such a structure would never be permitted under planning regulations.

The Municipal Hall site, early 1970s. This building, occupied today by Newcastle Library, was not always intended to serve that function. The building was apparently intended to be a supermarket but there were no takers and so the decision was taken to move the library here from School Street. Prior to School Street, the library had been in the Municipal Hall, which had of course been on this site before this building. The library was formally opened by Councillor H. Beet on 12 June 1975.

Nelson Place, around 1925. This view of Nelson Place was taken around 1925, as witnessed by the showing of the silent drama film *Afraid of Love* written by the Honourable Mrs John Russell. The scenario that Mrs Russell wrote was allegedly based on her own, bad experiences of married life. The building joined to the cinema was variously the Young Men's Christian Association (YMCA), Newcastle's first telephone exchange, and finally a shop.

Nelson Place from Barracks Road, 1961. This view was taken from the part of Barracks Road which, seven years earlier, would have been Bagnall Street. On the right are the swimming baths, complete with stained-glass windows, and below them a sign pointing to the library in School Street. Visible above the van on the left is Queen Victoria's statue, showing just how far out into Nelson Place it stood. No wonder it had to be removed when the roundabout was enlarged and the roads widened.

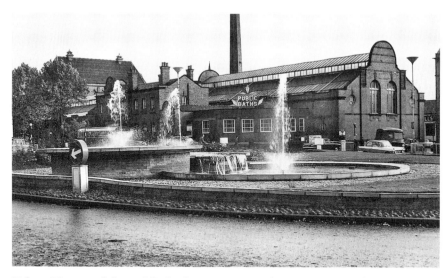

Nelson Place and the public baths, post 1963. This is a view of Nelson Place after the roundabout was enlarged and the fountains installed. Queen Victoria's statue had been removed to Station Walks and the cinema demolished. The Brunswick Street Methodist Chapel to the left of the baths, already closed for about six years, would soon be demolished. So, too, would the early nineteenth-century Nelson House, the end wall of which can just be glimpsed on the right.

Nelson Place/King Street, the old fire station, around 1965. This interesting view shows the remarkable miniature Georgian building complete with parapet, to which was attached the engine house of the fire station, with its large, red-painted doors. Next door was the Newcastle office of the Leek and Westbourne Building Society, which formed a stepping stone in the creation of the Britannia Building Society, now part of the Co-op Bank. The Leek and Westbourne Building Society existed between 1965 and 1975. (JWC)

Nelson House and statue of Queen Victoria, Nelson Place. Here the bust of Lord Nelson can be seen at the top of Nelson House. Completed by 1808, shortly after Nelson's death at Trafalgar, Nelson House was originally divided into two and later still was subdivided into three. Queen Victoria appears to be gazing up at Nelson, probably not amused that this public square had been named after him, a viscount, rather then after the queen and empress of half the world. (JWC)

J. Chadwick's olde curiosity shoppe, 13–17 Marsh Street, 1938. Chadwick's was well known and loved by antiquarians and collectors throughout the area. Not only is the shop now gone but so is the street that it stood in. Marsh Street ran from Nelson Place to Bath Street and the present civic offices would have stood in Marsh Street had it not disappeared by being incorporated partly into the Ryecroft dual carriageway and partly into Merrial Street.

H. Wheat's tobacconist, Bridge Street, 1930. Wheat's was located at the end of the building which Wain's chemists occupied from the late 1890s and Wheat's remained in those premises for nearly a century. As well as posters advertising smoking materials, there are also advertisements for Newcastle cinemas, one of them dating the photo to 1930. This road was variously High Street, Liverpool Road and Bridge Street at different times, but in this view 'Bridge Street' appears clearly above the name Wheat. (JWC)

Astons Furnishers, Bridge Street, mid-1960s. The three-storey building in the foreground was originally a fine eighteenth-century townhouse with extensive gardens. It was later converted into two shops, as here, one apparently called Regent House. Later still the shops were recombined into a large two-storey furniture store occupied by Astons of Wrexham. Finally it was occupied by Poundstretcher but was gutted by fire early in 2011 and the ruins later demolished. The A34 and St John's church are visible in the distance.

Bridge Street. This is a view slightly lower down Bridge Street than the previous image. This area always seems to have escaped the camera, except when Jimmy Wain photographed it here. These buildings were demolished in the mid-1960s and replaced by a block of shops with flats above them. The shops were originally occupied by retailers displaced by the demolition of their shops in Liverpool Road, including Bickley's tool shop and Brian Smith the jeweller.

King Street. This is the Congregational church in King Street, built in 1859 of buff brick with blue bands. Taken in September 1967, this photo also shows No. 8 King Street, which stood next door and was most unusual and striking. In 1839, No. 8 was owned by the Chapel Trustees and occupied by Revd William Chambers. Chambers was still living there in 1841 and the fact that it was the minister's house explains its proximity to the church. (JWC)

The Jolly Giant Building, 1990s. Starting life as a motor garage, this large sprawling building later became the Cee-n-Cee supermarket and then the Jolly Giant toy store. Today the site is occupied by No. 1 London Road, a block of apartments with an underground car park and its own gymnasium. In this photograph, posters advertise Tanita Tikaram and Barry White, whilst in the distance can be seen the much unloved Fine-Fare supermarket with its bright green and orange stripes.

4

BIG HOUSES

Maer Hall, 1850s.

Wherever there are plentiful natural resources and specialist skills, no matter how poor and ill educated a workforce may be, they have always succeeded in making large fortunes for their entrepreneurial employers. These men lived in grand – sometimes palatial – houses, some of which are pictured here. Sadly, many of them are no longer standing today.

Maer Hall 1850–1860. These first two photos of Maer Hall may be the earliest ever taken. Believed to date from the 1850s, they show the house around ten years after it was vacated by the Wedgwood family. From 1846, Maer Hall was owned by the Davenport family until they sold it in the 1890s to shipping magnate Frederick Harrison. Harrison enlarged the house by adding huge extensions to the west end.

Maer Hall, post 1897. This is how the hall looked with its extensions to the west end. The efforts made to add the extensions sympathetically are obvious, although there seems to be a slight discrepancy in the height of the main roofline. By the time Dr Tellright had them demolished in the 1960s, the extensions were apparently leaking like sieves and required tens of buckets to be put in place whenever it rained. No fewer than three covered swing-seats can be seen in this photo.

Maer Hall extensions staircase. This relatively modern photograph shows a newel post from the grand bifurcated staircase installed in Harrison's extensions to Maer Hall. The stairs were built and carved by Thomas Edwards & Son of No. 32 Ironmarket, Newcastle. Part of the staircase was purchased from Dr Tellwright by the Huntbach family and installed in the old Ebenezer Chapel in Newcastle when they converted it into a department store. The other surviving parts of the staircase grace a large house in Market Drayton.

Apedale Hall, around 1930. This is Apedale Hall standing empty and unloved before its demolition in 1934. Built by Richard Edensor Heathcote in 1826, the Heathcote family lived there until 1928, after which it was let to the manager of the Midland, Coal Coke & Iron Company. It later failed to sell and so was pulled down. Its two lodges, one contemporary with the hall and one later, still stand on Apedale Road, as do some of the other estate buildings, including the schoolhouse.

Thistleberry House; skating on the 'moat' around 1910. Thistleberry House stood at the junction of the present Thistleberry Avenue and Keele Road, in front of today's 'The Thistleberry'. In the rear garden a folly, known locally as Thistleberry Castle, stood on an island in a moat. Built by Samuel Mayer the folly was pulled down around 1919 and the bricks used to fill in the moat. This photo from around 1910 shows a man wearing a Tam o'Shanter skating on the moat watched by a young boy, possibly his son.

Brampton Hill House, the Brampton, around 1895. This superb photo by Edwin Harrison of Liverpool Road shows Brampton Hill House complete with its immaculately kept grounds, conservatory and stable block. It is a perfect illustration of the expression 'Where there's muck, there's brass' because the man who lived there in 1881 was Charles Massey, a 'rag and bone man' who rendered down dead animals to make glue, candles and artificial manure! It is now home to Synectics Solutions, a company providing 'innovative data driven business solutions'.

Trentham Hall, from the Italian gardens. Although Trentham Hall lay a short distance outside Newcastle-under-Lyme, as the major house in the area (lived in by the family who exerted most influence over Newcastle) it was felt essential to include it here. The hall as shown was the creation of Sir Charles Barry, architect of the Houses of Parliament. He took the existing early eighteenth-century house and by means of alterations and additions between 1830 and 1850 turned the house into a sumptuous Italianate palace.

Trentham Hall, dairy courtyard, 1920s. This Italianate clock tower, complete with its white-painted stone statue of Admiral Sir Richard Leveson (c.1570–1605), overlooks the Dairy Courtyard at Trentham. Sir Richard was a distinguished naval commander under Queen Elizabeth I, eventually earning the title Vice Admiral of England. The statue is a copy of a bronze memorial by Hubert le Sueur, in St Peter's Collegiate church, Wolverhampton.

Trentham Hall from West End. The grand west entrance to the hall enabled visitors to be guided along corridors and accomodated in parts of the house befitting their status. The porte-cochère bears the arms of the Duke of Sutherland with its wolf supporters. There is a well-known photo of King Edward VII and his entourage standing inside this porch but, by the time his son George V came here in 1913, although the porch had survived, the house hadn't.

The Firs, the Brampton, around 1955. The Firs was built in 1854/5 For Thomas Leech, maltster and cheese factor. It was later occupied by Stephen Edge, a corn merchant, then by the Moseley family (drapers) and was finally bought by Harry Scrivenor Adams, father of Boyce Adams, in 1928. After Adams' death, his executors sold it in 1955 to Newcastle Borough Council for £6,325. In 1956 it opened as the Borough Museum, home of the photographic collection from which this book has almost entirely been compiled.

Porthill House, Porthill. Porthill House was built by William Clowes in the late eighteenth century and is believed to be the house Arnold Bennett called Hillport House in *Anna of The Five Towns*. When sold later it was described as a family mansion, with thirteen bed and dressing rooms, billiard room, library, dining room, drawing room, lodge and brook feeding pools suitable for rearing trout (now in The Dingle). When sold in 1849 it was divided into two: Porthill House and The Grange.

The Limes, Porthill. The Limes was built in 1860 and was occupied by earthenware manufacturer Enoch Wedgwood from 1860–1879. In 1881 Charlotte Clive, proprietor of a flint mill, lived there and in 1911 it was home to Sydney Malkin, a wealthy encaustic tile manufacturer. The house was eventually converted into flats and then burned down, allowing the building of a modern housing development on the site of the house and grounds. This photo of the doorway was taken soon after the fire.

Basford Hall, Basford. Basford House, as it was originally named, was built around 1780 by William Bent, the Newcastle surgeon who had amputated Josiah Wedgwood's right leg in 1768. It was located at the end of a tree-lined avenue now called The Avenue and had extensive grounds. Some of the associated farm buildings still stand in the Norman Grove area. It had an attractive lodge at the end of the avenue (next photo) and became a children's home before being demolished about 1940.

Basford Hall Lodge, Basford, 1984. The lodge to Basford Hall stood at the junction of Etruria Road and The Avenue until the 1980s, even though Basford Hall itself had been demolished around forty years earlier. By the end of its life the lodge, originally a miniature version of the hall, had been much enlarged and the original structure is the further part with the tiled roof and triangular pediment. The site where the lodge stood remains vacant.

Butterton Hall. Butterton Hall was built between 1840 and 1850 by Sir William Pilkington but sadly was severely damaged by the army during the First World War and demolished in 1924. The ruins of this hall's mid-sixteenth-century predecessor still survive close by, as does the stable block, built at the same time as the later hall. The photograph only shows the more ornate part of the hall; to the left can just be glimpsed the edge of another large though less elaborate range.

St Lucy's PNEU School, Porthill, around 1960. Situated in a large house in Second Avenue, Porthill, St Lucy's was a Parents' National Education Union (PNEU) school, this organisation having been founded by a Miss Mason in the late nineteenth century. Having spoken to a former pupil, it seems that at least some of Miss Mason's subjects were still taught into the late 1960s when St Lucy's closed; these included 'Picture Study' and 'Shakespeare'. The motto of the PNEU was 'I am, I can, I ought, I will'.

Pitfield House, the Brampton. Pitfield House is one of the villa properties built on the Brampton for businessmen. It was built in 1853/4 for Henry Hall, a timber merchant whose business might still be said to survive because a timber yard has always been present on at least part of what were Hall's premises in Bagnall Street/Barracks Road. Having been run by the council as the arts centre at which interest groups and classes met, Pitfield House is now home to a nursery and café.

Moreton House, Wolstanton, 1973. Moreton House, originally called Wolstanton Hall, took its name from the Moreton family who lived there from at least 1743 until 1842. In the 1970s the house was suffering from rot and subsidence and so permission was sought to demolish it. Fortunately this was refused and instead it was taken down brick by brick, moved, and the front, sides and roof rebuilt around a modern apartment block on good foundations. This photograph shows the rear wing, facing Grange Lane.

Moreton House, Rear Range, 1973. This second 1970s view of Moreton House, taken from one of the nearby Borough Council tennis courts, shows the row of cottages that stood to the rear of the house – presumably former stables or a services range. A hopper on the guttering downspout bears the date 1743 and the initials of Ralph and Hannah Moreton. According to P.W.L. Adams though, the original house must have been there much earlier than this date.

Clough Hall, around 1910. Clough Hall was a large Georgian mansion built around 1802 by John Gilbert. Thomas Kinnersley, a Newcastle banker, bought it about 1813 and his family occupied it until 1879, when it fell into disrepair. In 1888 it was bought by Robert Heath who sold it to a consortium of businessmen, whilst still retaining control. It was opened as an amusement park in 1890 but failed within four years. It then underwent a series of short-term uses before being demolished during the 1920s.

Chesterton (Old) Hall, 1908. Chesterton Hall in Castle Street was a timber-framed manor house dating from the early seventeenth century. It stood near where Chesterton Community Sports College's swimming baths are today. Castle Road is so called because Chesterton's Roman fort that may have caused the name 'New-castle' to be necessary a thousand years later stood here. Thomas Pape excavated the garden of the Old Hall in 1925 but failed to uncover any signs of Roman occupation.

Keele Hall. Of the many photographs of Keele Hall, this is one of relatively few that show the hall as it appeared immediately following a major rebuild in the 1850s. A visitor reported that 'some of the ornamental details might have been better' and another went so far as to say that 'The Chinese tops to the turrets of the garden front are, to my taste heavy and ugly and the dome of the smoking room squat and fantastic'. These oriental accents were quite soon removed.

5

LOST HOUSES, LOST STREETS

Bell's Hollow.

This section contains images of a number of Newcastle streets that were demolished during the clearances of the 1930s, 1950s and 1960s. Images of these streets are scarce and most have come from the clearance area or compulsory purchase files kept by the Borough Council until they were released to the Borough Museum. There are also a few photos of more suburban or rural houses and streets that have been demolished.

Bath Street and Civic Offices from Salter's Lane, 1968. This rare photograph from a 1968 clearance area file shows the last part of Bath Street to remain standing after the civic offices were opened on 22 September 1967. The houses were demolished quite soon afterwards and the name of the street changed to Corporation Street. Bath Street, which had been in existence since 1840, was much longer than Corporation Street is today.

Bath Street, 1968. This second 1968 photo shows the fronts of Nos 30–46 Bath Street, complete with a street-name sign. The advertisement sign written on the wall is for Colin Smith's shop in Bridge Street. A member of staff at the shop photographed the surrounding area to record the changes that were about to take place when the ring road was built, and one or two of those photographs appear in this volume.

Salter's Lane around 1930. Salter's Lane ran from Bath Street in the north to Liverpool Road, which it joined opposite Northern Stores at the top of Bridge Street. Northern Stores can just be seen in the distance. When the housing in Salter's Lane was demolished, leaving just the shop on the junction with Liverpool Road, the street was renamed Hickman Street.

Liverpool Road from Broad Street, around 1963. This photo looking down Liverpool Road towards the town centre was taken from the end of Broad Street. It is one of a series of photos taken to document the changes made to the Liverpool Road area as part of a major road reorganisation in the mid-1960s. It shows, amongst other things, a small detached sports shop, beyond which was Salt's Funeral Directors and St John's church. In the distance, the large white building is Aston's Furnishers.

Bass off-licence on the corner of Broad Street and Foden Street, 1960s. This shot was taken from Broad Street, looking towards Liverpool Road. On the left, the Bass off licence is on the corner of Foden Street and next to the photographer is a former corner shop. The partial Wall's ice cream sign indicates the presence of a second corner shop on the opposite side of the road. The properties stand empty here awaiting demolition. Did the Ford Anglia belong to a tenacious resident, or was it perhaps the photographer's?

Hall Street, 1955. This photograph shows part of Hall Street, one of a group of streets of terraced housing located to the west of Upper Green. Hall Street still exists today but leads off Knutton Lane and ends at the land formerly occupied by Newcastle-under-Lyme College and now by Sainsbury's supermarket. Photographs of the original streets in this area are extremely scarce and in some cases non-existent, as far as is known.

No. 2 Mortimore Street, 1955. It appears that when this photo was taken all of Mortimore Street had been demolished except for the shop at No. 2. As the other streets in the area had also been demolished, one can't help but wonder – who was shopping here then? Mortimore Street ran from Upper Green towards where Ashfield's New Road is now and so would now be underneath Sainsbury's supermarket. The buildings next to the shop appear to be an old farm.

Bull's Bank. This may be the only photograph ever taken of Bull's Bank. Photographs entitled Bull's Bank usually feature the short alleyway leading to St Giles' Chuchyard with Bull's Bank itself disappearing to the left. This undated Pape photograph shows Bull's Bank during demolition (The same area is shown from St Giles' tower in Changing Scenery). In 1881 there were four houses in Bull's Bank, two occupied by Irish couples, one empty and one occupied by a married woman whose husband was absent but whose surname was Irish.

Old house foundations, Hassell Street.
This photo by the author shows foundations that were briefly exposed when the new Wilkinson's store was about to be built in Hassell Street. The old bus station was removed and stripping off the road surface revealed a number of these bases that had probably supported timber-framed buildings. It was normal to support wooden buildings on stone to prevent the beams at the bottom of the walls from becoming waterlogged and eventually rotting.

Bow Street, 1960s. Bow Street probably gained its name from the fact that part of it formed an arc between Hassell Street and Bagnall Street/Barracks Road, as can be seen here. Oddly, the row of terraces running out of shot to the left was also part of Bow Street, as was the street leading from the other end of that row to Hassell Street. Normally such an arrangement would be three separate streets. Bow Street was demolished in the 1960s.

Houses on Thistleberry Avenue, 1979. These houses on Thistleberry Avenue originally stood facing the houses on Keele Road (*see* next photo) across the gardens of Thistleberry House. Between the two rows of houses was the castle and moat (shown in Big Houses). These houses appear to have been altered somewhat on the right since being built, possibly to provide space for extending the Thistleberry Arms. Was the arch surrounding the door on the left once a coach arch giving access to the stables of Thistleberry House?

Houses on Keele Road, 1979. This short row of houses on Keele Road would at one time have had a pleasant view from their rear windows, because they stood quite close to the folly in which Joseph Mayer of Thistleberry House kept his collection of antiques and curios. Just over the rear wall/fence of these houses was the path that wound around the Thistleberry House gardens, within which was the folly and its moat (*see* Chapter 4, Big Houses).

Racecourse Cottages, Silverdale, 1930. Racecourse Cottages stood in the fork between Downing Street and Park Road, Silverdale. Today this entire area is a large residential development; Downing Street no longer exists and Park Road is lined on both sides by new housing. The two cottages on the left appear to have been suffering from subsidence as can be seen from the extensive work between the ground and first-floor windows. Not surprising, then, that they fell into a 1930s clearance area.

Rear of The Gothics, Silverdale, 1958. This rare view of the rear of The Gothics came from the Borough Museum's Clearance Area collection. Its proximity to St Luke's Church of England is quite apparent from this view. St Luke's was built in exactly the same period as The Gothics (1853). It has a broach spire, meaning that it is located on top of a square tower and has a number of facets or broaches.

Opposite above: **The Gothics, Silverdale, 1958.** The Gothics were stone-built cottages near St Luke's church in Silverdale. Built in the early 1850s, they achieved fame by appearing in the 1940 film *The Proud Valley*, starring Paul Robeson. Set in the Rhondda Valley, the film concerned black American David Goliath, who got a job down a mine and joined a male voice choir. Kent's Lane Colliery and The Gothics were made out to be in Wales and Robeson never actually visited Silverdale. The cottages were demolished in 1960.

Opposite below: **Cottages on Black Bank, 1959.** These cottages stood directly opposite the Methodist chapel (*see* Pick 'n' Mix) on the old Black Bank Road, the main road between Knutton and Alsager's Bank. When the area was open casted all the surviving cottages and the Methodist chapel were demolished and the road largely destroyed. A new, wider and faster road was built, although a short length of the old road – complete with its cat's eyes – still survives, now hidden in developing woodland.

Church Lane, Wolstanton, around 1960. On the right of this view is the New Inn, later The Archer and now the New Smithy. Of the five properties shown three are, or were, shops. To the left are Church Cottages and then St Margaret's church itself. According to records, the five properties shown here were listed for compulsory purchase in 1939 but this does not seem to have happened for another twenty-something years, after 1959. They have now been replaced by Saint Wulstan's Catholic Community Centre.

Church Lane, Wolstanton, September 1960. This row of four cottages stood opposite the end of The Archer pub. This photo was taken in 1960 and the cottages, like many other Wolstanton properties, appear to have been suffering from severe subsidence, probably as a result of the network of mine workings running underneath the area. All four properties had required some stabilising of the brickwork between the windows, always the weak point in walls subjected to subsidence.

6

FULL STEAM AHEAD

Canal Extension Railway from Friarswood playground.

The coming of the railway to Newcastle was a complex matter and there were eventually several railways built by different companies/consortia. The railways tended to be linked to their canal predecessors: the passenger line through Newcastle station was built partly over the old Upper Canal and another, the Canal Extension Railway, was built in order to carry freight to and from the Lower Canal, which terminated near the Boat and Horses pub in Brook Lane. The railway was to outlive the canal.

1901 steam locomotive *Newcastle*. *Newcastle* was a 0-6-0ST locomotive built in 1901 by Manning, Wardle & Co Ltd of Leeds. It was purchased for use by the Midland Coal Coke & Iron Co. Ltd at Apedale Ironworks. In 1916 it was loaned to the Ministry of Munitions, and then sold to a company of contractors in Wolverhampton. By 1927 it was put to use by the British Sugar Corporation in East Anglia, where it worked until 1969.

***Newcastle* arriving at Beamish Museum, County Durham.** Much later, the restored *Newcastle* was purchased by the Beamish Museum in County Durham. One could be forgiven for thinking that in this photograph it is passing through Sunderland on its low-loader but it is actually arriving at the 'town' in the museum created by re-erecting typical buildings of the late Victorian period, obtained from various parts of the North East. Beamish visitors might be upset to learn that this loco was not named after 'their' Newcastle.

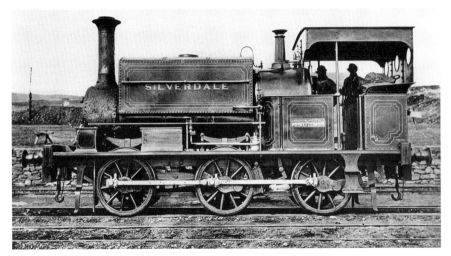

1868 locomotive *Silverdale*. This second Manning and Wardle 0-6-0ST locomotive is *Silverdale*, which was built around 1868 for use by the Midland Coal, Coke and Iron Co. Ltd. *Silverdale* may have been built alongside the first *Newcastle*, which was also used by that company. It appears that *Silverdale* was withdrawn from service about 1900, broken up and converted into a stationary winding engine at Silverdale Colliery, used for raising and lowering the miners' cages down the shaft. It was apparently still in use until the 1970s.

Pool Dam Coal Wharf, 26 April 1964. The Silverdale–Newcastle Railway was built by Ralph Sneyd to carry coal from his mines at Silverdale to the coal wharf to sell. Later the Canal Extension Railway was built to carry the coal onwards to the gasworks and to the Lower Canal near Brook Lane. The site of the wharf is now parkland and the former Silverdale line has recently been tarmacked and the trees thinned to transform it into a light, pleasant walkway.

Locomotive 47596 passing Friarswood School, 7 January 1965. Here Locomotive No. 47596 is passing Friarswood School en route to Blackfriars' Road. The man with the flag races ahead to stop the traffic, as there were no gates or flashing lights. On the left can just be seen the end of the corrugated iron St Peter's Mission church, used later by Friarswood for French lessons. No one could hear '*un mot*' the French assistant said when the locomotives thundered past. Trainspotting was second nature for Friarswood pupils.

Locomotive 44571 crossing Pool Dam, 17 October 1964. This locomotive is on the Canal Extension Railway, although by 1964 the canal had been out of use for more than forty years. This line was used to deliver coal from the coal wharf at Pool Dam to Newcastle gasworks and also to the canal terminus, near to where Homebase stands now. The railway crossed Pool Dam, Blackfriars' Road and Brook Lane. Here the locomotive is crossing Pool Dam, the man with the flag having stopped the traffic.

Crossing Blackfriars' Road, January 1960. This photograph taken from St Giles' Parish Hall shows the sheer size of this locomotive and tender, which dwarf the Ford Anglia van waiting for the train to pass. On the left the gap in the low wall is the entrance to St Peter's Mission. The skyline is unrecognisable compared with today, as virtually every building visible except St Paul's church was demolished within a few years of this photo being taken.

Empty train between Blackfriars' Road and Brook Lane, 14 January 1966. Here locomotive 78056, with empty coal wagons and its brake van, pass alongside the Lyme Brook between Blackfriars Road and Brook Lane. To its left, over the wall, was the cattle market car park, frequently used as an overnight lorry park, and beyond that the cattle market itself. Up ahead are the gasworks and gasometer, removed when the large Safeway supermarket (now Morrison's) was built on the area. Sadly no signs were uncovered then of the Black Friars' friary.

Empty train entering Brook Lane sidings. Brook Lane was different from the two other road crossings on the Canal Extension Railway, in that it was equipped with crossing gates to stop the traffic. Here the locomotive is shunting empty coal trucks into what was by then called Brook Lane Sidings for the night. In the background can be seen the gasworks and gasometer.

Newcastle station from the rear of a locomotive, 7 April 1962. This rather unusual photograph shows Newcastle station from a goods train between Newcastle station and the bridge carrying Queen Street over the railway line. Both platforms can be seen, as can the roadside building to the right and the covered ramp down to the platform on the left. Although the station is now a distant memory, the Borough Arms Hotel, built to cater for passengers arriving at the station, is still in business.

Locomotive 47596 at Liverpool Road halt, 29 July 1964. Originally called 'haltes', these miniature stations were unmanned and designed to help trains compete with trams. Liverpool Road halt was situated just north of Ashfields New Road and the trackbed and bridge under the road are still there, now used as a walkway. Having passed under the road, the track passed behind William Mellard's house – The Beeches – en route to Newcastle station. The stop was used by machinists making army uniforms at Enderley Mills.

Diesel locomotive B4 at Newcastle station, 7 January 1964. Although steam locomotives were still in use when Newcastle station closed, diesel locomotives had by then been in service for a number of years and did visit Newcastle station. Class 104 locomotives, like this one, were built in Birmingham between 1957–9 and perhaps surprisingly, the last were only taken out of use in 1995. Today the Churnet Valley Railway has restored examples of these, which are appropriate to the line, having mainly been operated in the north-west of England.

Silverdale station, 1964. This photograph shows Silverdale station with St Luke's church in the background. One door is marked 'Booking and Waiting' and the one at the near end is the 'Ladies Waiting Room'. Benches are provided outside for hardier passengers to wait on. The crates on the platform seem to contain 'empties' going back to a brewery somewhere for cleaning and refilling. The station finally closed to passengers between Silverdale and Stoke in 1964.

Track-lifting at Halmerend. This spectacular 1960s view shows rails, complete with sleepers, buffers and even weed-encrusted ballast, being lifted from the trackbed at Halmerend. The caterpillar tracked crane doing the lifting belonged to British Railways.

7

CHANGING SCENERY

A farm in Clayton.

This section contains a selection of scenes that are very different today from how they looked when the photographs were taken. Probably the single most important factor in bringing about these changes was road transport. The increasing number, availability and speed of cars and lorries meant that roads needed to improve rapidly: they needed to be wider, straighter and better surfaced. The effects of those changes to roads are clear in these images.

The White House, Clayton Road. This photo comes from the Tivey collection donated to the museum. Tom and Madge Tivey lived in The White House shown here on the right, close to today's Westbury Park mini-roundabout. The house still stands, although the surroundings are now very different. In this photo Clayton County Primary School stands next to the house, but was demolished many years ago when Clayton Road was significantly widened. Some of the school outbuildings still survive though.

Clayton County Primary School, Clayton Road. This photo from around 1964 was taken from outside Clayton County Primary School, looking towards Clayton Green. By this time the school was an annexe to Langdale County Primary School. The road here is much wider than previously but would later be enlarged to four lanes and provided with a roundabout at its junction with Northwood Lane and Westbury Road. Today's huge Westbury Park development was built on what had been farmland.

Zoar Village, Thistleberry Avenue, 1920s. This is Zoar Village on Thistleberry Avenue, looking towards Gallowstree Lane and Gallowstree Hill. The 1879 OS Map shows 'stump of tree' on the hill and this presumably refers to an alleged 'Gallows Tree'. It is difficult to reconcile this totally rural view with the built-up area it is now. In the 1960s this area was known as Thistleberry but has now elected itself part of The Westlands, with the beneficial effect that confers on house prices.

Zoar Village, Thistleberry Avenue, 1920s. Zoar Village is so-called because one of the pairs of cottages there has a plaque high on the wall bearing that name. The 'village' was built before 1818 on land owned by Reverend T. Massey and was named after the city to which Lot and his daughters fled from Sodom in the Book of Genesis. The religious community who made their home here presumably felt that this too was a place of peace and safety.

Gallowstree Lane, 1920s. Until the 1960s, Gallowstree Lane remained a rough track and was obviously a popular dog-walking location. On the left, below the tree line, can be seen a row of rifle targets at The Butts. This firing range must have been in use for at least half a century, with bullets passing through the targets and into the soft clay hillside behind. The entire area to the left is now a large housing estate centred on Paris Avenue.

Orme School. This undated photo of what was originally the Orme Charity School shows two of the cottages that used to stand next to it when it was built in 1850. The school was attended by Arnold Bennett, who renamed it Oldcastle Middle School in his novels. It survived as a boys' secondary modern school until around 1967, when the Edward Orme School opened on Gallowstree Lane. Friarswood School then moved into the building and when they left it became a community centre. At the time of writing, the building is up for sale.

Priory Road, shortly after construction, around 1930. Priory Road was cut through the sandstone at the edge of Friarswood around 1928. It provided a more direct route to Seabridge, Whitmore and beyond, and also helped the development of The Westlands. Here the concrete walls are complete and landscaping is under way. Later the terraces on both sides of the road would be lined with high-quality housing and, on one side, also the Society of Friends' meeting house. Friarswood Silk Mill is visible on the right.

Stanier Street around 1936. This interesting image could be described as homework. It is labelled in the museum archive as Stanier Street from Knutton Road, but for several reasons that description seems unconvincing. Poring over old Ordnance Survey maps has failed to reveal what is shown here, so perhaps this is a reader's opportunity to shine. Please contact the author or the museum if you can work out where this view was taken from.

Wolstanton Marsh and Marshlands cinema, around 1929. This 1929 view shows the large house standing today at the edge of Wolstanton Marsh, now hidden by trees. To the right can be seen the row of four cottages (*see* Missing Houses, Missing Streets) and further right, in what used to be Barker's Square, is the Marshlands Cinema. The cinema closed in 1960 but remained in situ for a long time afterwards. Where it stood is now a car park used by St Wulstan's School and patrons of The New Smithy pub.

View from St Giles' Tower, 1935. This fascinating view is one of several taken from St Giles' 90ft-tall church tower in 1935. It shows Holborn, on which can be seen Lamb's Paper Mill and various other businesses. D. Shenton's advertises itself as 'Haulage Contractor, Furniture Remover and Coal Agent' and at bottom right can be seen Bull's Bank, with its sign on the wall, and the small alleyway leading off it towards the churchyard. Holborn is now incorporated into the A34 bypass.

Blackfriars' Road. This busy view from the 1960s shows the busy junction of Priory Road, Blackfriars' Road and Friarswood Road at rush hour. The photographer would have been standing with his back to the Canal Extension Line still carrying goods trains at the time, the road-traffic here having to be stopped at intervals by the flagman (*see* Full Steam Ahead). The large building is St Giles' Parish Hall and behind that is Friarswood House.

Police station and Municipal Hall, 1960s. To repeat this view today, the photographer would have to be standing in the centre of the Ryecroft dual carriageway. The significant difference between the two images would be the complete absence of the Municipal Hall, possibly the reason why this 1960s photograph was taken; the start of the 'Muni's' demolition couldn't have been far in the future.

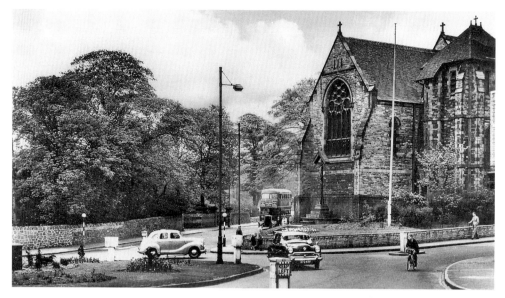

St Andrew's church Porthill. This 1950s view shows Porthill roundabout, and the north end of St Andrew's church, with its tower overlooking Watlands View. Some of the old boundary walls to the Watlands Hall estate still survive at the rear of the church and other buildings in the area. Today the church, built in 1886, is largely obscured by trees from this angle.

Minton Street, Wolstanton. This unrecognisable view shows terraced housing on the left side of Minton Street and part of Red House Farm on the right. In the distance is St John's Wesleyan Methodist chapel and to its right are terraced houses in Nelson Street, the only part of this scene unchanged today. Minton Street's terraces, the farm and the chapel were all demolished many years ago and today the scene is dominated by a small Asda supermarket and the new Morris Square.

8

PEOPLE AND EVENTS

Neil, Morris Square, Wolstanton.

This section contains a number of photographs of royal visits dating from 1911–49, together with other images where people, or one-off events, were the photographer's subject. These cover a wide range: from weather events, the effects of war on Newcastle, ordinary street scenes involving people and even family photographs that capture an occasion or bring to mind a certain period.

Effects of whirlwind at Clough Hall, Kidsgrove, 5 August 1911. Two months after George V came to the throne, a fierce wind tore through Kidsgrove and this photograph shows some of the damage it caused at Clough Hall. Presumably at that time there were no weather forecasters to reassure people that there was no hurricane coming.

Coronation procession, Penkhull Street/High Street, 1911. The quality of this photo is poor, but it may be the only one to survive of this event: the coronation procession of King George V in 1911. In comparison with other events in Newcastle it seems quite poorly attended, until you notice that Red Lion Square is thronged with people and that behind the top-hatted officials are several large coaches. Behind those coaches may have been thousands of townsfolk, as taking part in processions was almost obligatory in those days.

No. 4 Water Street, coronation celebrations. This family group stands outside No. 4 Water Street, Newcastle at the time of the coronation of King Edward VII in 1901. The plaque on the wall advertises Mrs H. (Sarah) Bramwell, who gave daily lessons in dress-cutting and shows that her establishment was either called the 'Cosmopolitan Dress-cutting Association' or was associated with that organisation. The elderly bearded gentleman was Mrs Bramwell's father, William Hand, who was 92 years of age at the time.

Betley royal visit. On 22 April 1913, King George V and Queen Mary were in the middle of a three-day visit to Cheshire and north Staffordshire. They stayed at the palatial Crewe Hall and drove through Betley without stopping, en route to civic receptions in Newcastle and Stoke-on-Trent. They later visited Trentham Park – the hall itself having been demolished the previous year – and Keele Park before returning to Crewe Hall in the evening.

Above: **Royal visit panorama, Nelson Place, 1925.** In 1925, King George V and Queen Mary visited Newcastle for a second time. There are many photos of their appearance in Nelson Place but this image is unique in that it shows the entire tableau. It was taken from the upstairs of Nelson House (*see* Town Centre) and it is possible to pick out Queen Mary on the dais, being presented with a posy by a little girl.

Left: **Princess Elizabeth inspects female Guard of Honour.** On 2 November 1949, Princess Elizabeth visited Newcastle-under-Lyme, just over two years before the unexpected death of her father George VI propelled her on to the throne. Here Her Royal Highness inspects a female guard of honour outside the Co-op Emporium at the bottom of the Ironmarket. It is not immediately obvious whether the guard were adult soldiers/airwomen or cadets. After this, Princess Elizabeth took tea in the Municipal Hall with the mayor, mayoress and other town officials.

Crimean cannon being removed from Stubbs Walks, 1965. This photo, one of a series taken to document the Crimean cannon's journey from Stubbs' Walks to the Brampton, shows the heavy bronze barrel with its embossed two-headed Russian eagle being craned on to a trailer outside the Orme Girls' School in Victoria Road. Girls from the school, mistakenly believing that the cannon was to be scrapped as the First World War tank had been earlier, protested and hung a notice on it saying 'Hands off our cannon'.

Opposite above: **Burke's Garage, the Higherland, 1930s.** Here we see a very sporty convertible obviously being admired by the staff of Burke's Garage on the Higherland. Interestingly the car carries a learner's L-plate, which were not introduced until 1935, just one year after the first driving licences were issued. The Automobile Association badge displayed on the radiator was current from 1930–39, all of which suggests that the photo was taken in the 1930s. In the background can be seen the junction of Union Street and Higherland.

Opposite below: **Boys playing on Crimean cannon, around 1940.** Here a group of boys, including a Milky Bar Kid impersonator, plays on the Russian cannon presented to Newcastle by MP Samuel Christy following the Crimean War (1854–1856). The cannon used to stand in Stubbs' Walks between the Orme Girls' School and Newcastle High School and from 1919–42 a British First World War training tank used to keep it company. The cannon was removed to the grounds of Newcastle-under-Lyme Borough Museum at the Brampton in 1965.

Corpus Christi procession, Grosvenor roundabout area. Here a Corpus Christi procession passes through on its way to Holy Trinity Roman Catholic church. The processors wear traditional Polish costume and may be the children of refugees from either the Nazis or the Red Army during the Second World War. In the background are the George Inn (*see* Newcastle Brown, Anyone?) and the row of shops on the left of Barracks Road, demolished in the 1980s so the road could be widened to four lanes.

Filming *My Fragile Heart* at St Margaret's church, Wolstanton, 2000. Filming for a major TV drama in Wolstanton is a big event, although it was kept so quiet that few spectators turned up to watch. *My Fragile Heart* was a two-part murder drama set in Stoke-on-Trent, but Wolstanton church obviously offered a better setting than churches in Stoke and so the cast and crew descended on St Margaret's. Huge lights mounted on scaffolding were fitted to the church to simulate the sun streaming through the stained-glass windows.

Filming *My Fragile Heart* at St Margaret's church, Wolstanton, 2000. These two 'priests', together with the rest of the cast, walked from St Wulstan's Community Centre car park where the caravans, make-up artists and catering van were parked; the only person who didn't walk was the star, Sarah Lancashire, who was driven the short distance in a sort of Popemobile. The author was only there because he had been told that Raquel Welch was being filmed (it was in fact Raquel Watts, *Coronation Street* character).

Flooding at Red Bull traffic lights, Kidsgrove, 1982. A dramatic photo of Red Bull traffic lights possibly in 1982. The driver of the lorry on the right is probably regretting his confidence that his vehicle could negotiate the water. The 2010 Draft Local Climate Impacts profile for Newcastle Borough describes the area as having a 'rich historical legacy of flooding' and, according to the Environment Agency's flood maps, it has a '1 per cent likelihood of flooding each year'.

Friarswood School, 1960s. Friarswood School in the 1960s was probably not a state-of-the-art institution, although it may have been no worse than many other schools. Mrs McLeod taught joined-up writing in this classroom and it is possibly her blackboard resting on its side, already prepared for the next lesson in penmanship. There would be no distractions caused by what was happening outside the windows, unless the pupils came to school equipped with stepladders.

Outside Friarswood School, 1960s. Children leaving Friarswood County Primary School on a cold winter's day in the 1960s. The lady nearly sitting on the bonnet of the Ford Popular is a teacher and carries an attendance register, which may indicate that it is only lunchtime and she is making her way to the old Fleet Air Arm annexe next to Harvey's shop on the Higherland. Today the Morris Minor would certainly not be permitted to park where it has in this photo.

Christmas at the Dog and Partridge, 1960s. This image is a snapshot of a family Christmas in the 1960s. Here Susan Wantling plays magnetic football against a man, possibly her grandfather, or just a privileged pub customer allowed into the inner sanctum. On the left, Susan's brother Robert spectates, probably desperate for his turn. The children's mum, Mrs Mavis Wantling, does not appear in the photo, possibly because it was she behind the camera. It would be interesting to see this décor in colour.

Robert and Susan Wantling outside Newcastle fire station. Here the children from the Dog and Partridge pose in front of one of Newcastle's up-to-the-minute fire appliances outside the new fire station in Knutton Lane. This fire station was built in the 1960s but has just been demolished and building has now started on a new performing arts facility for Newcastle-under-Lyme College. A new fire station now stands further along Knutton Lane.

Horse and trap outside St John's church, Liverpool Road. This photograph was taken by well-established Newcastle photographer Edwin Harrison, who had moved his studio from High Street to Liverpool Road in 1873. St John's church used to stand on the opposite side of the road from Harrison's studio, so he wouldn't have had to travel far for this commission. It is not known who the driver was but perhaps he just wanted a record of his new wheels.

Newcastle police station, Second World War. Newcastle's new police station opened on 29 February 1936, the move made necessary by the demolition of the old Roebuck building in High Street. That building had housed the former police station, at one corner. Here the new station, only a few years old, is impressively piled with sandbags covering the ground-floor windows. The corners of the piles have been painted white to make them visible during the blackout and to guide police officers to the entrances.

9

NEWCASTLE BROWN, ANYONE?

The Lord Nelson, Wrinehill.

This chapter looks at a selection of pubs in the Newcastle area, all but two of which are no longer standing. Newcastle was well known for its large number of licensed premises and no fewer than three of the pubs shown here were in one short street, Bridge Street. The first photograph shown is of the Lord Nelson in Wrinehill and is one of the earliest photos in the book, probably dating from between 1860 and 1890.

The Globe Hotel, 1950. The Globe Hotel was built in 1898 and was an early steel-framed building, handsomely decorated in terracotta including two half-globes in the gable. In the 1950s it closed as a hotel and was converted into a shop. The arched windows were removed, forming a covered arcade which allowed purchasers to browse the new inner windows in comfort (*see* Town Centre). It was demolished in around 1968, along with the rest of the row of shops, to make way for York Place shopping centre.

The Old Brown Jug, No. 19 Bridge Street. The Old Brown Jug is pictured here around 1900, when Mr William Walker was the landlord. Walker kept the premises between the 1890s and about 1910. The windows contain advertisements for plays including *When London Sleeps* (1896) and also one for Lester Collingwood's travelling troupe. Collingwood owned the Alexandra Theatre in Birmingham but also organised groups of actors to tour other areas, putting on plays wherever he could obtain a venue. He was sadly killed in a road accident in 1910.

The Old Vine, Bridge Street, around 1912. The Old Vine stood across the road from the end of Froghall and was demolished around 1970. This photo may show the landlord, George Rowe, in the doorway. As with the Jug, the windows acted as advertising space for local theatres, prominent amongst which was the Grand Theatre, Hanley. The Grand opened in 1898 and was converted to a cinema in 1932 before being destroyed by fire the same year. The Art Deco replacement Odeon is now the bar Revolution.

The New Vine. Although this is actually a family photo of a Corpus Christi procession in Bridge Street, it provides a very rare glimpse of the New Vine public house. The landlord at that time was David Spencer Jepson. When the pub closed it was dramatically altered but still stands today, occupied by the China House Chinese restaurant and takeaway. The ornate window lintels visible in this photograph still survive above the first-floor windows.

The Old Pomona Inn. The Pomona Inn – or The Roper's Arms as it was originally called – was created around 1867 as part of a large seventeenth-century house. This had been occupied by Samuel Bell, one of Newcastle-under-Lyme's few potters, hence the nightclub that later occupied the site being named Sammi Belles. Today many shards of Bell's delicate Pomona ware (1725–1755), including a complete Redware teapot, can be seen at the Borough Museum. The Old Pomona closed down when the entire building became The Placemate. Now the building has stood unused for many years.

Dog and Partridge. This photo of the Dog and Partridge at No. 20 Holborn was taken at the time of the coronation of King Edward VII in 1901. Kate Nee's name was above the door despite her husband John being listed as an innkeeper on the 1901 census. Higher up Holborn, on the corner of Lower Green, a tall building can be seen with an ornate curved gable-end. That building is the Plough Inn (*see* next photo). The Dog and Partridge survived much longer than either the Pomona or the Plough, finally closing its doors in the late 1970s.

The Plough. The Plough was located on the corner of Holborn and Lower Green (*see* street sign on the wall). This photograph comes from a set of three glass negative made in 1911, all of which feature in this volume (*see* previous photo and People and Events), despite having been cracked and repaired using sticky tape. The year is specified by the coronation procession posters stuck to the wall on the right.

The Sutherland Arms, Blackfriars Road, 1990s. Although not particularly old, this is the solitary photograph of this pub in the archives of the Borough Museum. Although the building shown appears to be 1930s in style, there was already a large pub on the site as early as 1900. There was a long bar at the rear of the building in which concerts and discos were held. Given the pub's name, it is quite likely that the Sutherland Arms once belonged to the Trentham Estate.

The George Inn, Well Street/Barracks Road. The nineteenth-century George Inn on the corner of Barracks Road and Well Street is another pub which many people remember well but relatively few seem to have photographed. The George was open throughout most of the twentieth century but was demolished in 1987 as part of the Barracks Road widening scheme.

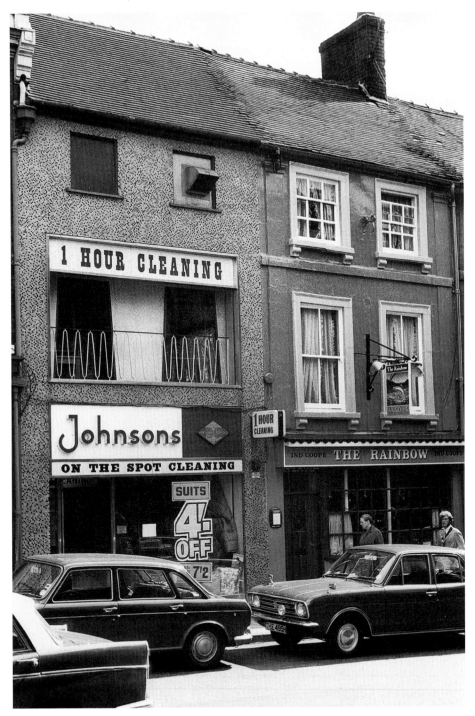

The Rainbow, High Street. Not many photos seem to exist of The Rainbow near to the market cross and certainly none as clear or as recent as this 1970/71 image from the Jimmy Wain Collection. The Rainbow first appeared as such in 1851, but the building itself dates back to the mid-seventeenth century and may already have been a hostelry under a different name. (JWC)

The Waggon and Horses, Higherland. This 1960s photo shows the Waggon and Horses pub on the Higherland. When it was built its nearest neighbour up Seabridge Road was probably Cheyney's Farm. Between the two were open fields (*see* Lost Villages), so the pub was literally on the edge of open countryside. Here the Off Sales Dept has been located inside the recently vacated Burke's Garage sales office. Burke's petrol pumps used to stand between it and the road.

10

PICK 'N' MIX

Queen's Gardens.

This final selection of images has been selected entirely at random and may appeal greatly to readers precisely for that reason. The fact that a lot of the images concern Wolstanton is pure coincidence and should there ever be a second volume in this series, it might just as easily contain a lot of images of another borough district.

Woodland Avenue, Wolstanton, October 1951. Here the dramatic effects of subsidence – probably the result of mine workings – can be seen clearly as one end of the attractive detached No. 1 Woodland Avenue Wolstanton is sinking gradually into the ground. The plank of wood next to the bay window indicates true vertical. This house, located behind the present Newell Palmer and Cameron Financial Services offices, was well beyond saving and had to be demolished.

Exterior of No. 101 High Street, Wolstanton, November 1938. This photo shows the rear extensions of No. 101 High Street tilting downwards at an alarming angle as comparison with the level piece of wood on the windowsill illustrates. New mortar below the window suggests an earlier attempt to repair the masonry but without success and the brickwork is once again being torn apart. This property was stabilised and is now the excellent and friendly W.S. Lowe's pharmacy.

Interior of No. 101 High Street, Wolstanton, November 1938. This is the inside of the same building as the previous photo. Here the floor inside the rear extension is seen to be sinking drunkenly into the ground. The bottles and barrel show that the building was already a pharmacy and that this rear space was used for distilling, mixing and bottling medicines.

George Hassell's family grocery, High Street, Wolstanton. George Hassells traded in Wolstanton for many years and is shown here, master of all, on the step of his shop, then No. 31 High Street. Now renumbered 91, this shop today is Wolstanton Hardware where, like Harrods, the staff will try to obtain any hardware or gardening item you might require. George is clearly eager to show how modern and well equipped his business is with its own horse and cart, well turned-out staff and delivery boy.

Dimsdale Parade, Hassell's delivery boy, around 1910. This slightly later photograph shows that George Hassell has now started to employ at least one young boy with a bicycle to make small deliveries. The boy shown is very smartly dressed (was this just for the photographer one wonders?) and the sign writing on the bicycle is very professional.

Minton Street, Wolstanton, May 1935. Dramatic subsidence is clearly visible at No. 22 Minton Street, where the window apertures have allowed for much greater movement than a solid wall would. This is probably not a house you would want to live in once it reached this state. Minton Street still exists, but not one terraced house survives there.

Pottery Headstones, St Margaret's churchyard. These ceramic headstones, with one for Thomas Pain who died early in the 1700s, were photographed in St Margaret's churchyard, Wolstanton. They survive today, securely mounted inside the porch. Originally there were many more due to the local population working in the pottery industry, who used clay as a way for people whose families could not afford stone headstones to be commemorated. Some are alleged to have disappeared, only to reappear in Liverpool Museum.

J.H. Shufflebotham's 'Newcastle Boot and Shoe Repairing Factory'. This building stood at the junction of Stubbs Street and Hassell Street near the entrance to the old bus station until its demolition in the late 1960s. Joseph Harvey Shufflebotham seems to have established his shoe-repair business here around 1915. This photograph was probably taken in 1932 or 1933 because one of the films advertised on the Pavilion Cinema Poster at the side of the shop is *No Greater Love*, which was released in America in 1932.

The 'Newcastle Boot and Shoe Repairing Factory' interior. Inside the shoe factory, several machines are run from belts driven by electric motors. The young boy is painting glue on to the bottom of shoes to allow the attachment of rubber soles. After Joseph Shufflebotham's death in 1935 the business was taken over by Charles Wainwright, a boy who had been taken in and trained by Joseph. When the shoe factory was demolished, the business moved to a new Wainwright's shop between High Street and Stubbs Street.

Midland Coal Coke & Iron Company offices, Apedale, 1960s. This building in Apedale, close to where Newcastle Countryside Project's base is now, was the offices of the Midland Coal Coke & Iron Company Ltd. The MCC&I Co. Ltd was formed in 1890 and owned a number of pits in Apedale including Burley, Bassiloes and Watermills and a number of others in surrounding areas. They also owned Apedale Ironworks and a coking plant. The large company finally failed as a result of the Great Depression of the 1930s.

Black Bank Chapel (undated). A primitive Methodist chapel, presumably this building, was registered at Black Bank in 1861. It was deregistered in 1940 and by 1957 was used as a barn. The chapel stood on the north side of Black Bank Road (opposite the row of cottages shown in Lost Houses, Lost Streets). It should be remembered that this is not the road used today, created after the opencast mining was carried out in Apedale, but the original Black Bank Road.

Brunswick Street Methodist Chapel. This imposing chapel was opened for worship in April 1861. As has happened with the majority of Methodist chapels in this area, the congregation became too small to justify keeping such a large, grand and expensive-to-maintain building open. It closed in 1956 and was demolished.

Ryecroft School. Ryecroft was an unusual and attractive school, built from yellow brick with darker bands and details. Built in 1874, it was the first school built by the newly formed Newcastle School Board and was located at the junction of Rye Bank and Croft Street. Although the road where it stood is now called Ryecroft, it wasn't called that between 1877 and 1900. The photograph of the boys' entrance shows that this was part of an 1890 rebuild.

Castle stonework, 1935. Newcastle's castle was built as a wooden motte and bailey around 1145 and was then surrounded by an extensive pool formed by dams at Pool Dam and Rotterdam. Later the castle was rebuilt of stone, but gunpowder rendered the castle useless as surrounding high ground put it at the mercy of artillery attack and so it had mostly disappeared by the sixteenth century. This photograph shows the beautifully cut and jointed stonework uncovered during one of several excavations carried out between 1904 and 1935.

Ivanhoe, Chesterton. This is an ideal picture for a final miscellany because it is totally unexplained, apart from the fact that this is the rear of a property at the rear of High Street/Audley Road in Chesterton. It is from a Borough Council clearance area file but there is no explanation as to what the name 'Ivanhoe' refers to – was it a pub, or is it the caravan? There were apparently no photos of the front of the building in the file and so that provides no clues either.

Municipal Hall stairs. This image will no doubt be upsetting to the many Newcastilians who remember attending functions of all kinds in the Municipal Hall. There are a large number of high quality images of the demolition of the 'Muni', both from inside and outside in the Borough Museum's collection.

Silverdale Co-operative Society bakery, Lower Milehouse Lane. This shows the newly completed Co-op bakery on Lower Milehouse Lane. It is a typical Art-Deco building, complete with its angular stained-glass window in the gable. It was built circa 1930 and was converted into the Normid Superstore, a supermarket run by the North Midlands Co-op, around 1980. It was eventually demolished when the present Morrison's supermarket was built.

The Tivey brothers. Published here, 100 years after the beginning of the First World War, this image shows the Tivey brothers in their North Stafford Regiment uniforms, prior to going off to fight in 'the war to end all wars'. Posing here they probably had no idea of the horrors that awaited them but thankfully they all came back alive. The connection between the Tiveys and Newcastle is that Tom Tivey and his wife Madge lived at the White House on Clayton Road.

W. and V. Clarke grocers, Higherland, early 1960s. This tarpaulin hooked over the window of the shop and bearing the proprietor's names is a throwback to a century or more earlier, when shops did not have plate glass windows as they do now. It was probably supplied by Betty Plant's and effectively turned Clarke's into an advertising hoarding whenever the shop was closed. The idea that sweets – put together out of so many different ingredients – could be 'pure' is somewhat laughable today.

Friarswood 'boys', 1960s.
This unusual photograph is of the inside of Friarswood boys' toilets which stood at the rear of the school on the right-hand side; they are just visible on the photograph of Locomotive 47596 passing Friarswood school. They were, of course, unheated and some very coarse, possibly horsehair, insulation can be seen just about encasing the pipes on the right-hand wall to prevent them from freezing in winter. A visit here was never a particularly pleasant experience.

High Street, Alsager's Bank. The changes between this photograph and the scene today are relatively small. The most obvious differences are that the small shop and café on the right and the large Methodist chapel in the distance on the left have both been demolished and replaced by other buildings. At the time that this photograph was taken the Farmer's Boy would still have been serving locals with beer, but today it is a private house and the nearest pub to here would be the Gresley Arms.

Opposite: **Rear of Hayden's/Woolworths in Penkhull Street, around 1940.** Another unusual view, this time looking over the yards of the timber-framed houses that lined one side of Friars' Street, towards Penkhull Street. The building occupied by Hayden's stood on the corner of Penkhull Street and Friars Street and was demolished before 1942, although the houses remained standing for another ten years. The large building to the right was part of the indoor market, which in its time served variously as an indoor riding school, roller-skating rink and council garage.

If you enjoyed this book, you may also be interested in...

Staffordshire Folk Tales

THE JOURNEY MAN

This delightful book is a collection of marvellous tales from the moorlands, Mercian Staffordshire, 'the middle' and the Black Country. These are the polished jewels of old Staffordshire, the stories that her people have held on to, even as they laboured for others in the factories and fired up the kilns.

978 0 7524 6564 7

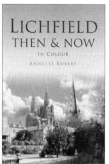

Lichfield Then & Now

ANNETTE RUBERY

Protective of its architecture and its customs, Lichfield nevertheless remains a modern city where old and new co-exist. *Lichfield Then & Now* pairs 45 carefully chosen photographs from public and private collections with 45 contemporary colour versions of the same views, providing a fascinating visual chronicle of the city's progress.

978 0 7524 6113 7

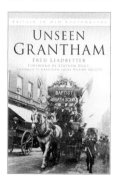

Unseen Grantham

FRED LEADBETTER

Unseen Grantham features 200 previously unpublished photographs and postcards that will appeal to everyone with an interest in the period of Grantham's history from the middle of the Victorian era until the 1960s. All aspects of everyday life are recorded here, offering a unique glimpse of a bygone time for all who know this Lincolnshire market town.

978 0 7509 5911 7

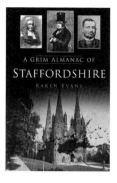

A Grim Almanac of Staffordshire

KAREN EVANS

Full of dreadful deeds, strange disappearances and a multitude of murders, this almanac is a day-by-day catalogue of 366 ghastly tales from Staffordshire's past. Including the young girl cut to pieces by a machinery explosion, the tragic deaths of 155 men in the Minnie Pit disaster of 1918, and the theatre performance where the gun really did go off, mangling the actor's hand and causing a severed finger to fly across the stage, read it only if you dare ...

978 0 7524 9902 4

Visit our website and discover thousands of other History Press books.

www.thehistorypress.co.uk